What People Are Saying . . .

If you are struggling with your health, or know someone who is, you will be inspired by Janell's miraculous recovery. Allow it to build your faith!

Janell Price and Raymond, her husband, are longtime family friends of ours. In fact, I was once their pastor. Alice and I have admired their walk with God and each other. We were shocked the day we heard that Janell had received a diagnosis of cancer, and immediately signed up on Facebook to help provide prayer support for her.

I remember the dark days of their struggle as their faith was tested. You see, individuals don't get cancer, families do. It takes a toll on every family member. We were elated the day we heard she had received her miracle. Since she is a writer, I'm not surprised she is using her passion for writing to share her passion for God, and the story of her miraculous healing.

--Eddie Smith,
www.USPrayerCenter.org

Janell is a testimony to the miracles that only God can perform. I have known her professionally for years and have seen her walk this difficult journey. She is truly a woman of grace and is a reminder to us all of HIS healing. This book touches the soul and heart as she shares the account of her journey with cancer.

--Dr. Andrea Wilson, *D.C.*
Kerrville, TX

As I read Janell's book, I was impressed by a number of things. First, her faith-in-God persistence to stand on the Word of the Lord, "You will not die but live," and live she did. Next was the faithfulness of those in her inner circle. They proclaimed the truth of God's ability and experienced that it was so. Finally, I was captivated by the flow of encouragement that comes in reading her story. If you want to see what a faithful God will do, this book is a must-read.

–Jack Rothenflue
Director, Commission To Every Nation USA
International Mission Sending organization)

The most sincere, heartfelt story of complete faith in God I have ever read.

--Marjorie Price
Neighbor

Janell is living proof of God's divine provision for healing. Her absolute intention to stand on Psalm 118:17 no matter what the circumstances, is a powerful testimony of faith and persistence - qualities God loves.

We are all blessed and encouraged to "go and do likewise" when the storms of life and cancer, in particular, seem insurmountable. Thanks, Janell, for sharing your miraculous story, and we declare the power of this testimony! YES, LORD, DO IT AGAIN!

--Richard Holcomb
Leadership Team,
Impact Christian Fellowship, Kerrville, TX

There are times in our lives when we all need a miracle. What we may not realize is that they are all around us. Not in just the beauty of the creation, but in the beauty of the neighbor that you may have never met. Janell's story is one of these miracles. The beauty of her faith will inspire you and the beauty of God's faithfulness will comfort you with His Mercies.

To God be the glory.

--Lisa Motes Johnson
Teacher, Fayetteville, N.C.

Janell, with Raymond's constant loving support, has faced a stack of situations that were at times overwhelming. But true to His Word, God provided the way for her to stand up under all these things. Her life is a testimony and an encouragement. Through the hard times of sickness and recovery, Janell kept finding her way into God's grace being sufficient for all her needs.

It is my joy to pastor the fellowship where God planted Raymond and Janell the last several years. They are both a blessing. I hope you experience the Lord's goodness as you read *Healed of Cancer: Journey to a Miracle*.

One of the things we often talk about is the power of testimony. We like to say, "Testimony means do it again, Lord God." As you read, may you experience the power of the Lord's grace made perfect in weakness, as well as the joy that is always ours in His presence.

--David Danielson
Pastor, Impact Christian Fellowship
Kerrville, TX

HEALED

OF

CANCER

Journey to a Miracle

By
Janell Price

Copyright 2017

Janell Price, Kerrville, TX 78028

Cover picture by Briana Schulze

Gardencarrot@gmail.com

All rights reserved. No part of this book may be reproduced without prior written permission of the copyright owner except by a reviewer who wishes to quote brief passages in connection with a review for inclusion in a magazine, newspaper, or broadcast.

Printed in the United States of America

7710-T Cherry Park Dr, Ste 224
Houston, TX 77095
(713) 766-4271

Paperback: 978-1-365-87340-9

Hardcover: 978-1-387-05754-2

DEDICATION

This book is dedicated to my husband, Raymond Price, whose love, faithful goodness, and wisdom helped me through the rough patches of life, especially the near fatal one covered in this book.

I am forever grateful!

My heartfelt thanks to our family and all the intercessors who stood by me in prayer. You made a difference!

CONTENTS

What People Are Saying i
Dedication vii
1. How It Started 1
2. Years Later 5
3. More Lumps 9
4. A Happy Birthday 13
5. Bad News at Home 15
6. Chemo 17
7. From Bad To Worse! 21
8. Treatment Reaction 23
9. No Place Like Home 27
10. How God Built Faith 29
11. Do It Again, God! 31
12. Raymond's Story 33

1.
How It Started

Many families are touched by cancer. For me and mine, it was melanoma — the dangerous kind that spreads aggressively through the body, sometimes after being surgically removed. I had three surgeries over a period of time and the melanoma came back stronger every time. It became metastasized melanoma, also known as Stage IV Melanoma. These quotes from the Internet explain it better than I can:

"What is melanoma? Melanoma is the most aggressive type of skin cancer. While melanoma accounts for less than 5% of all skin cancers, it is responsible for a large majority of skin cancer deaths." http://about.com

"Stage IV melanoma means that cancer cells have spread beyond the skin and regional lymph nodes to distant organs such as the liver, lungs, brain, or distant lymph nodes and areas of the skin." http://cancercenter.com This photograph shows a typical melanoma.

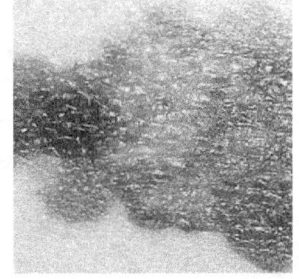

Photo by Wikipedia

My experience with skin cancer started almost 30 years ago. I didn't know it was skin cancer, and neither did the first three doctors who looked at it. Each dismissed the itchy mole-looking oddity behind my right elbow as having no importance.

Time passed slowly. One night a sharp pain near my right elbow woke me, so I examined the area. In the middle of the "mole" was a dark shiny spot. It was hard to see because it was on the back of my arm, so I hadn't given it much thought, especially after a string of doctors dismissed it. But now that it was hurting, I became alarmed and made an appointment with another doctor right away.

When I saw the new doctor, she took one look at the hurting growth and said it must be removed immediately. She called a surgeon she knew, told him what she suspected, and he agreed to see me right away.

Even though I was a stranger to them, they were both anxious for me and wanted me to go that minute for immediate surgery! I had to say no because my young daughter would soon be getting off the school bus at home with no one to greet her or unlock the door for her. So I set up an appointment for the next morning.

Out-Patient Surgery

The doctor recommended to me was a dermatologist. When I got to his office I found it full of patients, so the wait was long. But this doctor was so concerned for me that he gave up his lunch hour to remove the growth.

He was very thorough. The surgery took a full hour. There was just the two of us, and I was wide awake, so I took advantage of the time to ask him all the questions I could think of relating to skin problems. He answered me good-naturedly, but he also told me that I was in denial about the seriousness of my condition. Ouch! Obviously I wasn't ready to deal with the new reality of my situation!

I was given information on how to care for the wound from the surgery. Soon I got a call to come to the doctor's office. He had sent a biopsy of the tissue to M. D. Anderson, Texas Medical Center, and the results were back. I was afraid, but I was hoping for the best.

Once I was in the office he got right to the point: the tissue analysis came back positive for melanoma cancer. I was shocked.

I had a follow up appointment later at M.D. Anderson where we discussed possible treatments. There I was told that if I went 10 years with no reoccurrence of melanoma I could consider myself out of danger.

A new drug trial was about to start, and I was offered a place in it. The conditions made it impossible for me to participate. First of all, I would have to commit to be there once a week for several months until the trial was over regardless of how I felt.

Secondly, there would probably be side effects, so I would need someone to drive me, stay at the hospital while the test drug was administered, and then drive me home.

Since there were no assurances this trial drug would be beneficial, and I had no one to drive me both ways during the day, I opted out of the trial. No other treatment appropriate to my condition was available at that time at M.D. Anderson.

M.D. Anderson - Photo by UTMDA1" -Zereshk Own work. Licensed under CC BY 3.0 via Commons https://commons.wikimedia.org/wiki/File:UTMDA1.JPG#/media/File:UTMDA1.JPG

2.

Years Later

Why am I writing this now, decades later? Because several years ago I had a growth appear under my right arm. Although alarmed, I was comforted when the ultra-sound showed it to have "no signs of malignancy." As the months passed, it continued to grow despite my faithful use of a supplement recommended by my physician. The growth became so large that surgery was necessary.

The surgeon did another ultrasound with the same results as earlier: "no signs of malignancy." I asked him if he had noticed on the Patient History form that I previously had a malignant melanoma skin cancer removed on the same arm. Despite that, he guaranteed me the growth was not malignant. My second guarantee!

The surgery was no big deal but the aftermath was. I have a history of reacting to meds, especially if they cross the "brain barrier."

There was a list of everything I had ever reacted to on my hospital bracelet. But I had never been exposed to morphine.

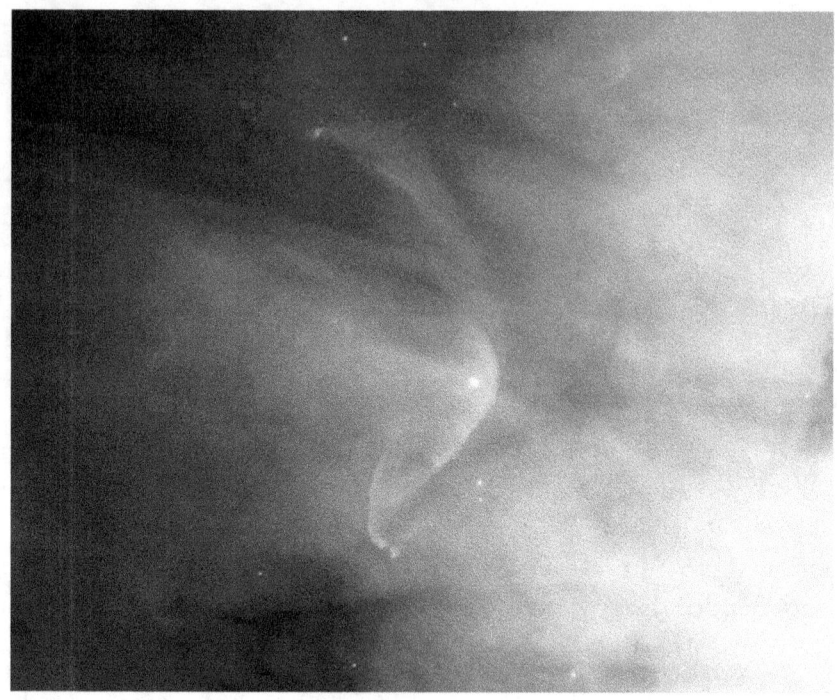

Photo by NASA (Public Domain) via Wikimedia Commons.

The more morphine pumped into me, the stranger I felt, like I was traveling through space. From my perspective, the room was definitely moving!

Oddly, although it did nothing to stop the pain, it affected me in another way. From far, far away I heard an other-worldly voice ask, "What is your pain level, from one to ten?" I answered "Seven." The voice kept asking that question, and I kept giving the same answer because the pain did not diminish.

Finally, despite my impaired condition, I had the good sense to say, "No more pain medicine, no more!" Inside, I was crying out to God for help.

Suddenly I saw visitors standing around my bed. They were all dressed in white tunic-like garments over jeans.

Healed of Cancer

Sitting in a chair next to my head, dressed in the same kind of attire, was someone who looked like my deceased mother.

These beings carried on quiet supportive conversation with me. To this day I can't remember a word of it. After a while, because I was very weak and tired of all the talk, I said to them, "You aren't real -- you need to leave." They left but soon came back and continued talking to me quietly, apparently with the double intent of keeping me sane and awake.

My surgery was supposed to just be "day surgery," but the head nurse was not going to let me go home unless I could walk. Despite dizziness, weakness, and disorientation, with my husband Raymond's help and that of the mysterious visitors, I was able to walk out of the hospital.

Much later I realized my white-clad visitors had been angels, and I felt bad for rebuking them for talking! I am sure angels are not usually that talkative, but I believe, in answer to my prayer and that of others interceding for me, the angels were strengthening me so I could go home.

Was that really my mother seated next to me? I wasn't sure. My theology didn't have an answer for that question.

Christmas was approaching, and we were delighted to have our daughter Mary and her husband Sean with us for the holidays. Sean is a very "handy man," with many different skills.

One day as he sat looking into my kitchen, which was quite a few years old he said: "I can put in a new kitchen for you while I'm here if you want." After making sure that was how he wanted to spend his vacation, we agreed.

What woman wouldn't want an updated kitchen? I was delighted! Mary was our "shopping assistant and coordinator," and a neighbor loaned us the tools. Raymond helped where he could. And so it all came together. Despite my pain, it was one of my most memorable Christmases, topped only by the first Christmas we had with our oldest child, Scott, after years of barrenness. (But that's a story for another time.)

Because it took a while to recover from the surgery, I didn't schedule the required follow-up visit with my doctor right away. What was the hurry since I had been assured twice my growth was not cancer? Before I was ready, the doctor's receptionist called and asked that I come in. I still didn't think I had anything to worry about. But I was wrong. It was hard for the doctor to tell me, but the required lab test on the tissue he removed came back metastatic melanoma. For some, it is a death sentence. But I didn't know that then. I just knew it was serious.

Much later, writing this article, I looked on the Internet and found this statement on http://WebMD.com -- *Although in most cases metastized melanoma can't be cured, treatments and support can help you live longer and better.*

Time passed and one day while I was resting in bed, I heard a loud voice speak these words from behind me: "You will not die but live, and you will declare the glory of God." I knew immediately that there was an angel in the room bringing this message, although I did not see anything.

I learned later that those words are found in Psalm 118:17. The angel's words quieted my soul and brought faith to me and assurance that I would live.

3.

More Lumps

Lumps appeared two more times under my right arm in the same place as when I first learned I had melanoma. Surgery was necessary again. The second time I had surgery I made sure I did not have morphine. Because of my past history of over-reacting to prescription drugs, I asked for no pain meds except to be allowed to take two Ibuprofen.

Unlike the first surgery, I awoke with no after-effects except some manageable pain that soon felt better after I took the Ibuprofen.

A Special Journey

When the lumps re-appeared for the third time, Raymond and I were RVing in California and on the West Coast. *(Photo on right)*

Bethel, CA was our main destination because we heard the Christians in that city had declared it a "no cancer zone" and were having great success in seeing those they prayed for healed of cancer.

We were especially interested in Bethel Church since the pastor there is a repeat guest speaker at our home church.

Also important were visits with family. On our way to Redding we stopped in Los Angeles to visit with our son Christopher, his wife Jenny, and their four children. Their friend Jennifer Pitts and her two children were present. Meeting Jennifer was important because she partnered with my daughter-in-law Jenny to pray for my healing. (More on that later!)

After our arrival in Redding, Jennifer, her husband and their two children arrived and stayed in the same RV park where we were already camped. We enjoyed visiting with them, and it was a blessing to see someone we knew at the church services. Not that people at Bethel weren't friendly - they definitely were, especially the students at Bethel's Supernatural School of Ministry. They were always ready to fellowship and pray for someone in need.

I especially enjoyed the prayer house at Bethel. It was open 24 hours a day with soft worship music playing continually, creating a healing atmosphere. One special night we attended a worship event there featuring hand drums and other percussion instruments.

Photo by Brenda Darnell

Added to this was the beautiful view through the wrap-around windows of the prayer house. Bethel is at a high point in the city of Redding, located between the Cascade Mountains and the Trinity Alps.

Healed of Cancer

The stunning snow-capped mountains can be seen from this special house.

In addition to hanging out in the prayer house, we attended Bethel Church services at every opportunity and also took advantage of other activities such as the Saturday Healing Room Ministry.

We attended a couple of classes, and I had several sessions at their counseling center, which I found very helpful. I'm still in touch via Facebook with the counselor I saw there. She and I have also done sessions on Skype.

Both Raymond and I attended a seniors' breakfast meeting. At that time, we had been in Redding almost three weeks and had not had an opportunity to meet the pastor, Bill Johnson, because he was always surrounded by a crowd of people.

At the senior breakfast I noticed him alone, leaning against the back wall. I went over and introduced myself to him, telling him I was a member of Impact, a church he has often visited and preached in.

I explained why we were in Redding and asked Him to pray for me. He very graciously prayed a faith-filled prayer for me. Did it make a difference? Only God knows. Bill praying for me was a desire of my heart, and I'm glad that desire was fulfilled. There were many people who prayed for me, and stood with me. I'm grateful for each one of them!

While at Bethel I saw this beautiful painting by Brianna Schulze that called me to take a leap of faith, cast off darkness, and step into God's glory. I was able to purchase a print of the original painting.

Brianna not only gave me permission to use it, but she also graciously provided me with the digital file to use as the cover illustration for this book. She has other paintings and can be reached at *Gardencarrot@gmail.com*.

This painting is also special to me on a personal level, because the girl looks very much like I did at age 15 when I met 18 year old Raymond Price. We married when I was 20 and he was 23. We have now been married 50 plus years, have three children, three "bonus" children by marriage, and eight grandchildren.

4.

A Happy Birthday

We arrived at Redding in early March 2011 and stayed three weeks, which meant on the calendar it was officially spring. However, it was still winter in Redding. I had never experienced such a cold and challenging winter!

One Sunday in late March as we left church, we had to step carefully through about three feet of what looked like tiny hail. It wasn't fine enough to be snow, so that is my best guess. Despite ice on the ground, I hoped to go north to Florence, Oregon to spend my March 27th birthday with my sister and her husband, Carolyn and Allen Krecker. But there was a weather advisory not to go north.

Allen suggested I check the Internet for traffic cameras on Interstate 5 North. When I did, I saw that the roads had been cleared and traffic was moving but ice and snow were piled up elsewhere.

About that time someone new pulled into the RV spot next to us. He lived in northern Oregon but had wintered in Phoenix.

Our new neighbor was pulling out to go north the next morning, and said he made the trip every year at this time. He was sure the roads were okay. So we headed out.

Texans like to say that everything is bigger in Texas, but we had never seen anything like the wild, wide rushing rivers of Oregon, or the rugged coast-line there! The small white structures on the point in the picture below belong to the Heceta Head Lighthouse.

The best thing about this third stop on our western adventure was having a reunion with my sister.

We spent a lot of time together discussing many things that brought emotional healing to both of us. (Many people think emotional healing also brings physical healing.)

Photo by Bruce Fingerhood, https://creativecommons.org/licenses/by/2.0

The second-best thing about this stop on our western journey was seeing the Heceta Head Lighthouse sitting on the Pacific Coastline. The worst thing was discovering that I once again had lumps under my right arm.

5.

Bad News at Home

My oncologist had approved our trip, but told me to be back by a certain date for more scans and blood tests. On our return home I quickly had the tests done. The results were very, very bad -- the melanoma had spread throughout my body into my lungs, liver, and even into my bones.

Raymond and I had gone over the options available for treatment for melanoma before, but now my doctor added something else: a new drug had just been released for the general public, specific to melanoma: Yervoy. She had been selected to use it on a test group and was familiar with it. But the public release had just happened, and we didn't know if it would be covered by Medicare and our insurance. If not, the cost would be out of our reach.

When I heard the bad news of the widespread melanoma in my body, especially after the encouraging atmosphere I had been in on the West Coast with family and friends and at Bethel Church, I went through a rough time emotionally. I shed many tears and wrestled with God for several days, reminding him He said I would live and not die. And now, despite that promise, death was staring me in the face, a very painful death.

At some point during my ordeal - I don't remember just when - I was on my back porch and spied this very special flower. It was shaped like a cross and reminded me of the promise God had made to me.

Someone I respected, who was concerned about my downward spiral, told me that wrestling with God wasn't wise. I thought of Jacob in Genesis and continued to wrestle until I got my faith back. I realized that the dangerous place I was in didn't change what the angel told me, which was that "I would live and not die." I determined to simply believe those words.

Photo by Janell Price

Remember my visitor in the hospital who came with the angels and looked like my mother? I saw her again in a dream. (At least I think it was a dream.) This time I saw a picture in my mind of her in my living room. She, my daughter, and I were standing together in my living room, as if in prayer.

My daughter Mary, who lived some distance away, had been asking to come, but I felt so bad, I was saying "No" to everyone who wanted to visit. For one thing, I did not have the strength to make conversation. And more importantly, I didn't want any tearful "good-byes" to weaken my faith in the word of healing God had given me. But the dream/picture with my mom and daughter changed my mind about my daughter coming. She did come and was a strength and a blessing to me.

6.

Chemo

Raymond, unknown to me until after I was healed, searched the internet about my condition and about the chemo my doctor offered. He was dismayed to read that the average benefit of Yervoy at that time was estimated to be only an additional 6 months of life. He didn't tell me that until I was healed, for which I am grateful! (I understand Yervoy is still being used today in conjunction with another drug with better results.)

Yervoy works by revving up the immune system. I started the treatment as an out-patient and found it tolerable. It was administered as an infusion utilizing an IV. The standard protocol at that time was four treatments, one every three weeks, with less-frequent boosters after that.

The treatment center was pleasant, with a multitude of big windows that let in natural light and allowed those of us receiving treatment to see outside. IV's were administered as we reclined in comfortable padded lounge-type chairs. The nurses were kind and attentive.

The patients were a diverse lot, as were the treatments. We often fellowshipped with each other and compared notes, or shared about our families and our "other lives"- the ones we had before we became cancer patients. It was almost like we belonged to the same private club. Almost, but not quite!

Magazines and books were available. At the back of the room were freebies that had been donated specifically for the cancer patients. Many boxes of new wigs of various colors and styles were in the back corner. At the front of the area was a hat rack with various styles of hats and scarves on it.

Also, available for the taking were some books, games and other items that didn't interest me so I've forgotten what they were. We could select whatever items met our needs.

I had understood that with Yervoy I would not lose my hair so I didn't expect to need the head-covering items. My hair is a unique shade of red. Raymond has always loved it and said that was what attracted him to me. He has a dry wit, and after decades of a happy marriage, I know there's more to our relationship than that, so I suspect he was teasing. But I still didn't want to lose my hair! I wasn't sure I would feel like me without it, but I found when I began to lose my hair I wasn't devastated after all. I was okay! I was still me!

I looked at every wig in the treatment room but didn't find one with a hair color like mine. So instead, I covered my semi-baldness with simple hats like this one.

Some of the female outpatients wore artfully arranged scarves to cover their increasing baldness.

I admired the effect, but despite several attempts, I couldn't get the knack of it.

Hat Photo by WikiHow

I had a lot of support. Raymond was extremely helpful. My family, church, and friends stood by, praying for me. I put together a private group on Facebook of Facebook members who were praying for me, and I posted updates as things progressed.

Being a writer, I am a person of words but I find it hard to convey how important this support from family and friends was to me. These wonderful people not only encouraged me with their posts and messages, but I am sure their petitions on my behalf were heard in Heaven.

Some days, especially as the cancer grew, I wasn't up to visits or even talking on the phone, but I could read messages on my iPod.

7.

From Bad To Worse!

The tumors continued to grow, and I began to decline. At that time I was still being treated as an outpatient and living at home.

It was my habit to walk every morning and evening in our beautiful rural community in the Texas Hill Country. A day came when I had trouble breathing on my morning walk. So I was put on oxygen 24-7. That worked for a while, but not for long. I was soon gasping for breath even with the oxygen.

I called my doctor and she offered immediate surgery, a dangerous surgery on my lungs with no guarantees. Raymond and I talked it over. Our understanding was that all that could be accomplished would be a short excruciatingly painful extension of life.

We prayed and took time to seek and know God's will. The result was that we had peace to not have the offered surgery. We understood that others may have made a different choice, but that was ours.

Because I was exhausted and struggling to breathe, I stayed in bed and concentrated on taking one breath at a time. That's all I could do. That and pray silently. Talking took too much effort.

I can't say I prayed beautiful prayers or made strong faith-filled declarations.

All I had strength for was to remind myself and the Lord of the angel's words that I would live and not die, and that I would declare His glory.

(Ps 118:17).

Photo by Angelo Juan Ramos, https://creativecommons.org/licenses/by/2.0/

Good News: Tumors Gone!

Something wonderful happened! As the days passed, I became aware that the external tumors under my right arm were shrinking. They had been very large and extremely uncomfortable, making it difficult to sleep. Now, every morning, I could see they were becoming smaller, and in three weeks they were entirely gone. ALL GONE!

Shortly after, I went in to see my oncologist and showed her my perfectly smooth underarm, now absent tumors and asked her, "Have you ever seen anything like this?" And she said, "No!" The nurse was quick to proclaim: "You got a miracle!"

8.

Treatment Reaction

*View from my backyard,
Photo by Janell Price*

I wish I could say that was the end of my troubles, and that I returned to a normal, healthy life enjoying the company of family and friends and the view from my back porch. However, that didn't happen. I had a severe reaction to Yervoy. It acted as a host to an unusual and extreme case of ulcerative colitis. We didn't know at first that was the problem. I became so nauseous I couldn't retain any food or drink. Various treatments were tried but nothing helped.

In that state, I quickly lost over 50 lbs. On my best day, I could only nibble on one or two boiled eggs throughout the day. I considered myself well-off if I could keep any of that down. Things got worse instead of better. I collapsed and was hospitalized. Our son Scott was quick to come. He and his wife Kelli both work in health care and were very helpful and supportive. Our daughter Mary stayed in touch by phone. She had come for a visit earlier.

At first no one knew what was wrong with me. A gastroenterologist was called in who was quick to recognize the source of the problem and begin proper treatment. I was in the hospital for a month the first time I was admitted, and then went back and forth between there and a nursing home several times. Raymond spent part of every day with me.

When I first went to the Nursing Home, Raymond and both our sons were with me. Scott was a good resource since he had worked in a Nursing Home. And so was Christopher, since he is a lawyer. For my peace of mind, I asked him to look over the contract Raymond and I had to sign before I was admitted.

Christopher's wife Jenny didn't come in person but she stood with me in prayer (Chapter 10), as did Scott's wife Kelli, our church, neighbors, and friends. I was surrounded by strength. It was encouraging!

Street clothes were required at the Nursing Home, and mine didn't fit because of extreme weight loss. Christopher solved the problem by buying me a new wardrobe. He was a good shopper, and thoughtful enough to also buy me a clothes hamper. I went to the Nursing Home grateful and well equipped.

For most of my time at the hospital I was fed intravenously while in bed in a hospital gown. Before being transferred to the nursing home, I was switched to ordering from the menu, while still in bed. Mostly I ordered Boost in a milkshake. I no longer cared for real food.

At the nursing home, it was a shock to be awakened at an early hour, dressed, and wheeled into the dining room where I was expected to eat real food, be upright and sociable.

I was no longer the morning person I had once been. (I still haven't regained that although I do enjoy real food now!)

Time passed slowly, typical when confined. I was shuttled back and forth between the hospital and nursing home for three months.

Swans on Scenic Valley Lake

I was a patient who wasn't very patient. I missed my valley home and the beauty of the hills that surrounded us, the deer that came at night, our little lake, the ducks, and the occasional swan or two (One year we had seven swans!).

9.

No Place Like Home

The third time I was scheduled to go back to the nursing home from the hospital. Raymond, who had spent time with me every day, spoke up and said he thought he could provide better care, and he wanted to take me home.

We were told I would not be released from the hospital to go home unless I could walk unassisted, something I had not done for three months. The day before my hoped-for release, a physical therapist came and worked with me. I amazed myself by being able to walk under his direction up and down stairs. My "performance" wouldn't have earned any rewards for style. I did it shakily, but I did it, and the therapist signed off for me to go home.

Once home, my strength began to return. Sometime afterward, I went to see the gastroenterologist who had diagnosed ulcerative colitis at the hospital for a follow-up exam. After checking me out in his office, he said "When I first saw you, I said to myself, 'this person is dying.'"

Once again, God chose life for me!

Six Years Later

After one year of clear scans, my oncologist told me, "You would be dead now except you got a miracle."

She continued to do routine scans for three and a half years and nothing unusual showed up. Now at six years out from cancer, I am only going in for a physical checkup and blood work once a year. Yeah, God!!

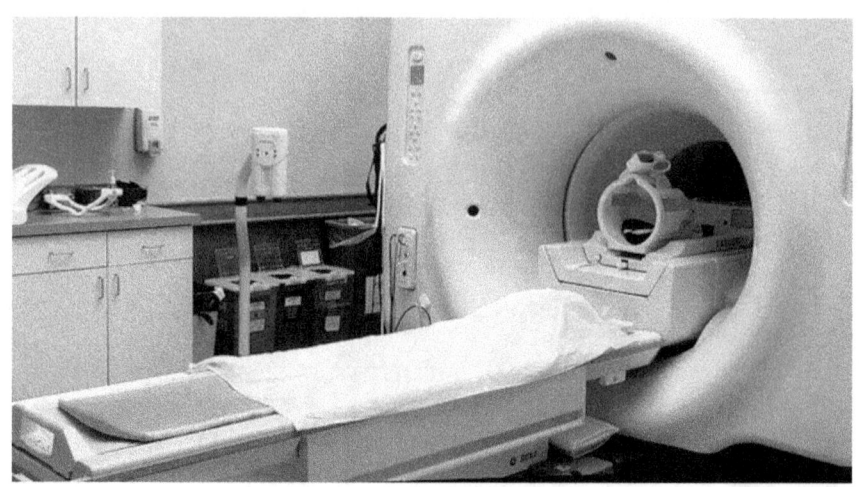

Photo by Liz West @ https://creativecommons.org/licenses/by/2.0/

Earlier, when I looked up the scripture the angel spoke to me, I found the phrase, "declare the glory of God" from Psalm 118 is sometimes interpreted as "publish the glory of God." Since I am retired from a career in publishing, it seemed a natural thing to do and is why you are reading this.

10.

How God Built Faith

Many people rallied around me to pray, including family, friends, past pastors, church intercessors, Facebook friends, and Healing Room ministers. Some spoke into my life in ways that brought faith, and I am thankful to them all! Since Hebrews 11:6 tells us that it is impossible to please God without faith, I am grateful to the "faith-builders" in my life!

Following is a testimony from my daughter-in-law Jenny about how God built her faith as she stood with me for healing. The Mary she refers to is my daughter, and Chris is my son, Jenny's husband.

I want to share what God did to maintain faith for your healing even when there were no outward signs of healing taking place.

On December 29, 2010, after you got your PET scan results, I called my friend Jennifer Pitts to pray with her on the phone. The most powerful thing we were both left with was, "We will believe the report of the Lord." After the call, I sat down to read my Bible (I was reading in Amos). I had an impression of Mary with child and I felt God say that "sign" of your daughter Mary with child would be a sign of your healing. I wrote it in my journal, and I shared it only with Jennifer. I wasn't sure if it was my own hope or God speaking.

MONTHS later, on June 5, 2011, Mary sent word she was pregnant. I then jumped up and shared with Chris what I had heard and had been holding on to for six months. That was before there was any sign that the tumors were shrinking. Much to the contrary, you were struggling increasingly to breathe even though on oxygen.

That sign was enough for me. Jennifer and I continued to pray in faith for your healing, bringing before God the things He had already said and shown to you, and to us.

Six weeks LATER you shared that the tumors had begun to shrink. And of course, that was before the second part of the battle for your life began. But for me, that sign from God was unmistakable - and gave me great conviction that your healing was coming. It helped me pray in faith through the darkest days, with a KNOWING that I can't explain, other than as a gift of faith.

I can't even describe the joy that rose up when you shared about the tumors shrinking. Your battle was still far from over, but at that point I had seen enough and heard enough that the enemy's taunts to cause unbelief would not stick.

11.

Do It Again, God!

So, what can I say in conclusion? I'm home, I'm alive, and I'm cancer-free!

Tests have decisively shown, and continue to confirm five years later, that I have absolutely no signs of cancer. Doctors have declared me a walking miracle, and my oncologist doesn't want to see me for a year. How affirming!

Impact Christian Fellowship

I am happy to be able to attend my church again! Our elders, pastors, intercessors, and friends at Impact encouraged us, prayed many prayers for us, and gave Raymond and I needed spiritual and emotional support during our journey to a miracle.

My pastor says giving a testimony means, "Do it again, God." So, my hope and prayer is this: "Do for others, Lord, what you have done for me!"

12.

Raymond's Story

This picture was taken on our 25th wedding anniversary. It's the last professional picture we made. We are at 53 years married now and counting. I wish we had made one on our 50th, but we were still dealing with the aftermath of chemo.

In 2010 our lives were changed forever when Janell was diagnosed with metastasized melanoma cancer. It was a very sad and scary time. So we began to pray as we had never prayed before.

One day while she was praying, Janell was told that she would live and not die. This was wonderful news that gave us faith to believe for a miracle.

She was operated on twice, and both times the melanoma came back with a vengeance. Eventually it was in her liver, lungs, and even her bones. But the worst thing was it had filled up her lungs. At that point, she had to have constant oxygen in order to breath.

Family, neighbors, and friends rallied round us to pray and help. We also received a lot of support and encouragement from our local church and prayer groups. Janell had a private group on Facebook made up of Christian friends from all over the U.S.A. and one in Canada. Many were from churches we had attended in Houston and kept in touch with. Some were "cyber" friends Janell had known for a long time, even before Facebook.

In addition to praying, some from these groups spoke words of faith and encouragement to us that were in agreement with what the Lord had told Janell: that she would live and not die.

Redding, CA

In the spring of 2011 we packed up and headed to Redding, CA and to Bethel Church. On the way we stopped and visited with our son Christopher, his wife Jenny, and their children near Los Angeles. We received much prayer from them, and from their friend Jennifer Pitts and her family.

The atmosphere at Bethel was faith-building and many good things happened there, but no healing was evident. From Redding we went to visit with Janell's sister Carolyn and her husband Allen on the Pacific Coast in Oregon and received prayers from them. We also prayed for them according to their needs.

On our return trip we stopped in Los Angeles to visit and pray again with Chris and Jenny. We headed back to our home in the Texas Hill Country carrying many prayers and good wishes with us.

When we got back, Janell's doctor informed us that a new treatment for melanoma called Yervoy was available. The cost was $600,000. We were relieved to discover that Medicare would cover it. Yervoy sounded promising, and we were excited that it was available.

Healed of Cancer

Tumors Disappear

After a couple of months, the tumors under her right arm began to disappear. She had a PET scan that showed no cancer anywhere. I thought, "Boy! That Yervoy is great." We visited the doctor and showed her the tumors were gone from Janell's underarm area. She agreed that she had never seen anything like that! Later she said it wasn't Yervoy, that it was a miracle. Since she had been having trial groups with Yervoy for several years before it was released to the general public, we knew she was qualified to make that judgment.

What great news! But soon Janell could not keep anything down when she tried to eat. I took her to the Emergency Room a few times but nothing changed. In that condition she lost 60 lbs and had to be hospitalized. She then spent time in a nursing home. Although we have friends who enjoyed their stay there, her experience was not good. Finally, I said, "No more nursing home! I can take better care of her at home."

She was able to rest better and to eat more at home. We travelled to Kansas City to see our eighth grandchild, Michael, just after his birth, and stayed there a couple of months. After getting home, Janell began having trouble keeping food down again and was put back in the hospital for 10 days. Eventually, she gained back her strength and weight.

We are so very thankful for the healing of melanoma! At the same time, Janell still needs restoration from the complications of chemo. But thank God she is alive, and is cancer free!